Hands of Years

Hands of Years

Poems by

Riley Bounds

Cover design by Shay Culligan

ISBN: 978-1-63980-037-7

Kelsay Books
502 South 1040 East, A-119
American Fork, Utah 84003
Kelsaybooks.com

Acknowledgments

I'd like to thank the original publishers of the following poems.

"Canticle." *Adelaide Literary Magazine Year III—Number 14—July 2018*, edited by Stevan Nikolic, Adelaide Books, 2018, 206.

"Canticle." *Ashvamegh Magazine*, April 2018, https://ashvamegh.net/2018-issues/march-xxxviii/poetry/riley-bounds/. Accessed 11 Mar. 2021.

"Cass." *This Present Former Glory: An Anthology of Honest Spiritual Literature*, edited by Matthew E. Henry, A Game for Good Christians, 2020, 140-142.

"Chapel." *Ekstasis Magazine*, 25 Oct. 2020, https://www.ekstasismagazine.com/poetry/chapel. Accessed 11 Mar. 2021.

"Commemoration." *Heart of Flesh Literary Journal Issue Four—November 2020*, edited by Veronica McDonald, Heart of Flesh Literary Journal, 30-31.

"Doxology." *Adelaide Literary Award 2018 Poetry Anthology*, edited by Stevan Nikolic, Adelaide Books, 2018, 145-148.

"Dusk Hymn." *Heart of Flesh Literary Journal Issue Four—November 2020*, edited by Veronica McDonald, Heart of Flesh Literary Journal, 31-33.

"Father." *Adelaide Literary Award 2019 Poetry Anthology*, edited by Stevan Nikolic, Adelaide Books, 2019, 292-294.

"Father, Again." *Ekstasis Magazine Issue 07*, edited by Conor Sweetman, Ekstasis Magazine, 2020, 29-30.

"Ketamine Prayer." *Anser Journal*, 6 Dec. 2020, https://anserjournal.org/rileybounds. Accessed 11 Mar. 2021.

"Mother." *Adelaide Literary Award 2019 Poetry Anthology*, edited by Stevan Nikolic, Adelaide Books, 2019, 291.

"Nocturnal." *Anser Journal*, 6 Dec. 2020, https://anserjournal.org/rileybounds. Accessed 11 Mar. 2021.

"On Death." *Amethyst Review*, 30 Dec. 2020, https://amethystmagazine.org/2020/12/30/on-death-a-poem-by-riley-bounds/. Accessed 11 Mar. 2021.

"Prayer." *This Present Former Glory: An Anthology of Honest Spiritual Literature*, edited by Matthew E. Henry, A Game for Good Christians, 2020, 137.

Contents

...my heart and I have not once lived as long
as May, and in my past life
there are only a hundred Aprils.
—Vladimir Mayakowsky, "A Cloud in Trousers"

Canticle.

At the tail end of the earth
there's some landfill
of songs and screams
that were
all carried
in the jaws
of strays
and buried where
our relative
inclinations,
ennui,
meet the cosmic
and sift into
the aurora
ebb,
and it's still lost
on me
whether I'll
remember
from the pirouetting
particles
the glass
I've crushed
underfoot
or the futility
of every
levity,
cadenza,

but I doubt
I'll mind
since all strays
die alone
anyway.

On Death.

In the space
where life
either bleeds
through linen
and strings
on tile
or faces
melt
through tables,
or in the space
where life
simply
leaves,
vagabond
through zodiacal
clouds
and dust,
there's no place
left for messengers.

Commemoration.

In memory of Nabeel Qureshi.

The whole world
tried to find you
by cigarette
light.
The apologists tithed
for an argument,
the pastors
lined up
to get
their wool
sheared.
The priest looked up
and saw blood
on the crucifix
for the first time,
or is it tears?

You can't leave now,
I've finally got
questions.

Did someone ride
with you
out there?
Was the lightning slick?

You shook
the eastern province
when they saw the star
falling up,

and the men
were thrown off
qibla
when the Kaaba
cracked.

A boy found an old hymnal
on the back of the pew,
and it finally made sense
before his mother
told him
not to sing
at funerals.

Buddha dropped by
to let me know
it only felt like pain,
no one needs
a stomach
anyway.

They marked up
your books,
and I can't help
feeling guilty
when I preach from them
on street corners.

If I see your wife
at the service,

I'll remind her
that nobility
shares a house
with eternity,
and that you
were the
noblest
of all of
us.

Cass.

Went to the blacktop
the other day
to count
the shards
of glass
on the shoulder.
Saw
the cursive
scream
of tires,
the abraded
kiss
of metal
on concrete,
ash like bumps
in black
acrylic
on the asphalt.
Cigarette butts
dropped by
the officers
who know the dead
don't mind
two hours
in the fire.
Me and broken
glass
on the street side.

Saw an angel
on a rock
with a
wire saw

crying
as he tried
cutting off
his wings.
Let me
take the saw
from him,
set it aside.
Sat in
his blood
on the rock
with him.
Didn't say
anything.

Thought of
how she
lit
my summer,
then the street
at night,
now the humble
sun
haloed
in our
ambivalent
sky
like her back's
to us.
We both watch
her steady
light,
her silent

swaying
fire.
She watches
Someone
beautiful
beyond us.
Me and the angel
watching her
dance,
all our lives,
all our
worlds
in her very
nature.

Now she's
a little
higher
than both
of us,
little
higher
than
all
of
us.

Nocturnal.

Bit my thumb
hard enough
to draw blood
and dragged it
along the side
of a building,
mark where
I've been.
Felt the wall
give and cave
like the ribcage
of something
that only
hates,
and I've walked
so far
now
that I don't know
if I have
the energy
to follow it
back.

Mother.

I'm sure one day
I'll crawl back up
one more uterine
hell
and wait
in the blood
and amnion
for
our hearts
to beat
together.
I'm sure
of
a lot
of
things.

Father.

You didn't
call me
about the
rapture
today.
Twenty-six years
of any day
now,
how everyone
would
pay,
and I don't
know
how to tell
you
I don't
think
God will save
us
from what's
already
happened.
But rant,
shout,
break your voice
against my
head
and let me
hear it,
because I'd rather
shiver in
your noise
than stand in

your silence.
Your heart
was always
a war
drum.
So stay
and tithe
your noise.
Stay,
and maybe
one day
gravity will
reverse,
all our ash
will fall
up,
and all the world's
fires
will spiral
into the upper
atmospheres
like jet
streams,
and all
that'll be
left
on the ground
is
what's
pure.
All our traumas
happened while
the sky watched,

so let's give it
hell,
let's give it
a taste,
you and
me,
whatever gives you
war,
whatever keeps you
fighting.
Keep
your dogs
this side
of memory.
Keep watching
for pale horses
and holes
in the sky,
listen for
the eagle,
just don't
stop
talking.

Father, Again.

Dreamed we
stamped out fires
in a smoldering
home.
You told me
you were proud
of my tribulation
heart,
just don't trust
every one that's
bled.
Hugged me
as our dead dog
bayed outside,
and then I woke
to the truths
whispering in
my ceiling.

Ketamine Prayer.

I followed
the arc of rainbows
and found
the pool
where all the
water
stops
and their prism
corpses
float
bloated
like any other
gray
dog
brought out
by
the sun.

Chapel.

I've burned a lot of chapels,
but I left this one standing.
Particles lilt and descend
in the sanctuary
like slow manna,
the thought of snow
and providence.
There's no ground
past the stained glass,
the cave of holy beasts,
hollow atrium
waiting on the promise
of an impulse.

There are three souls
here with me;
they carry
no words
in their briefcases,
they clothe
their eyes
and teeth.

The chapel faces east;
the sun
is threaded
through four
windowpanes
intersected by
a cross.
By four panes
we wait
for movement

through glass
and such resplendence
that we shed
these atoms
and find
valence
in the speaking
Light.
By four panes
we wait
for lift.

Doxology.

The hillside child
stands hanging on
every pulse
of clouds,
mouthing
the language
of lightning.
This is
the Ur Text;
this is
the Father
of Nations,
though the child
doesn't know
the name.
Thunder's heartbeat
throngs through
the arteries
of arroyos,
the ventricles
of canyons
below him
and breathes
on the fluid
morphemes
of rivers.
See the child
now greatly alone,
looking
to the stars
caroling
cosmic,
the cuneiform

of constellations
and the
tiny thunder
of his ribcage
proffered
to
Who he doesn't
know
from the textless
hymnal
of his solar
plexus,
the liturgy
of bone
and marrow.

What can he
say?
Dandelions die;
even the prayers
of birds
get caught
between
atmospheres.

The child raises
a hand
to the sun
softly burning
in the celestial
cathedral,
the moon
in

transit
menorah,
and extends
himself
to the unknown
Known,
the Painter
of the primordial
acrylic
so textured
as
to be
alive.

Dusk Hymn.

In the space between
a risen and set sun
I see Him
dance,
joyful in
the rift
of yesterday
and tomorrow.
Against
the equatorial plane,
I watch Him dance
with the sons
mothers forgot,
watch Him spin
with the girls
fathers lost,
watch Him step
with the untimely
ones
and raise
the little ones
in tiny
flight.
The light
and dusk
canvas Him,
and in
the great contrast
He never casts
a shadow.
In each pirouette
there's a smile
for each

dancing partner,
special for
them,
innumerable as
the dust
clinging to a
mother horizon.
And in
the semicosmic
movement
He smiles
for me,
the smile
my father
never could
and the smile
my mother
never gave
me.

He waves
me on.
I am
a dancer
now.
He waits
for me,
and for
the first
time,
I find
the feet
to walk.

Prayer.

Hope one day
I hold
the hands
of years
and become
the voice
I sing,
echoing up
the wall
of our
netted
souls,
refracting
each other's
given
light,
and in light
given,
and being
given,
singing,
and in singing,
be.

"In as far as you advance in love you will grow surer of the reality of God and of the immortality of your soul."
—Fyodor Dostoyevsky, *The Brothers Karamazov,* translated by Constance Garnett

About the Author

Riley Bounds was raised in Alex, Oklahoma. He holds an MA in Philosophy from Talbot School of Theology at Biola University and a BA in Creative Writing from the University of Central Oklahoma. He plans to continue into doctoral study. He lives in Norman, Oklahoma.

He is Editor in Chief of *Solum Literary Press* and its imprint *Solum Journal,* an annual literary journal. Solum Press is a Christian small press which publishes fiction, poetry, articles, homilies, and visual art. Learn more at www.solumpress.com.

www.ingramcontent.com/pod-product-compliance
Lightning Source LLC
Chambersburg PA
CBHW031155090426
42738CB00008B/1344

* 9 7 8 1 6 3 9 8 0 0 3 7 7 *